Tables and Graphics Explained

Making Your Placement Picture Perfect

Dr. Timothy Haupt, Psy.D.

Acknowledgements

I would like to thank my wife, Mariss, for her unflinching support.

Thank you, Nathan, Aaron, Jeremy and Joshua for giving me inspiration.

Thanks to my mom, Vera; who has shown me that stubborn is not always a bad thing.

Jackie Ryle – You have been my cheerleader through many years.

Rhonda Rhodes – You believed in me and encouraged me during some really bad times. Thank you for the mug.

Ilene Calderon – She has been a positive influence and encouragement in my work online.

Elaine Giuliano – Her belief that I am smart gives me encouragement to try even harder.

Andrew Gruttadauro – Thanks for the good words. Where's that cigar? I prefer Cuban Seed.

Never forget that believing in someone
doesn't do the work for them.
Your belief gives them a great reason for doing it.

Copyright Information

Illustrations:

Illustrations used in this booklet are purchased royalty free from the following web sites:

1. http://www.123rf.com/

Ideas

These web sites generously share their ideas.

1. www.word.tips.net

2. www.jegsworks.com

3. http://www.ehow.com/how_4798205_rotate-flip-image-ms-word.html

Trademarks

Note: If you find errors on this booklet, please send corrections to drtlhaupthhh@gmail.com . You will earn brownie points for your efforts and maybe a cookie.

ISBN-13: 978-1467932523

ISBN-10: 1467932523

COPYRIGHT: 1-683787971

1st *Edition*

Printed in the United States of America

Before You Begin

This booklet assumes you have a basic understanding of Word Processing and Spreadsheets. If you are not familiar with either concept, you should study up before completing the work in this booklet. Try using the free tutorials at:

http://www.microsoft.com/
or http://word.tips.net/

This booklet also assumes that you know how to save a document and create folders. If you do not understand these concepts, there are many resources on the Internet that are designed for you to get up to speed in those areas. I suggest Jan's Illustrated computer literacy:

http://www.jegsworks.com/

What this booklet IS:

This booklet is designed to give you a basic understanding of what tables in MS Word 2007, 2010 are, how they function, what features are available and how you can use this in the workplace. Additionally, this booklet explores the insertion, placement and formatting of graphics. At the end of the text, we explore a few intermediate functions and how they can help you.

Through exploration of the features in MS Word, it is hoped that you will experiment with the different tabs and groups as this is the best way to understand the use of your product in the workplace.

Introducing: The Ribbon!!

The Ribbon is the basic navigational tool that Word 2007 and 2010 use. Functions are grouped together in a logical manner called tabs.   Inside each tab is a set of groups. **Gone** is the traditional menu system in MS Office 2007.

Fig 1 – File > Edit Menu.

When you open an MS Office Program, you see the Home tab.   The Home tab has the following groups: Clipboard, Font, Paragraph, Styles and Editing.

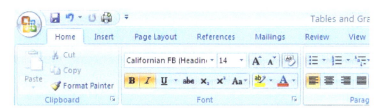

Fig 2 – The Microsoft Ribbon – Office 2007

Fig 3 – The Microsoft Ribbon – Office 2010

Tasks are accompanied by contextual tabs. Contextual tabs are usually a different color than the standard tabs and have tools available that help with design, layout or format of content.

Task	Additional Context Tabs
INSERT TABLE	Design and Layout Tabs
INSERT ILLUSTRATION(S)	Format Tab
INSERT HEADER OR FOOTER	Design Tab

Introducing: Tables

What are tables?

There is a table of contents at the beginning of this book. A Table contains information in a very specific and consistent format. Information can therefore be retrieved by the reader consistently.

Tables are groups of rows and columns. A row goes all the way across and a column goes all the way down. Put rows and columns together and you have a table.

	This is a caution symbol with an earth graphic in the center.
Fig 4 – A Table	

Columns and Rows

Just remember:

A Row is all the way across
A Column is all the way down.

A ROW IS ALL THE WAY ACROSS					
First Name	Last Name	Address	City	St	ZIP
Mike	Flabbier	1234 Boulder	Salinas	CA	93901
Tom	Blubber	1235 Boulder	Salinas	CA	93901
Fig 6 – Rows and Columns					

(left vertical label: A COLUMN IS ALL THE WAY DOWN)

A **Column** goes all the way down.

A **Row** goes all the way across.

Inserting a Table

Step 1: select the "Insert" tab.

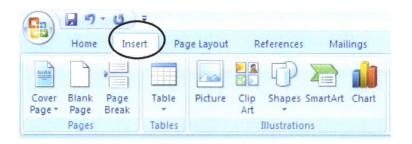

Step 2 – Select the "table" button in the "Tables" group.

Step 3 – Select the configuration of the table.   In this case, select 4 columns by 4 rows.

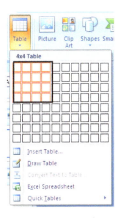

Select a 4x4 table using the 'Table' Button

After you click the left mouse button, you should have a table that looks like the one below:

A 4x4 table

Moving a Table

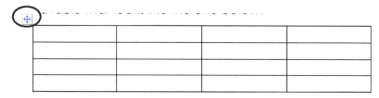

Fig 11 – The table with its handle showing

With your mouse hovering over the table, a handle appears at the top left hand corner. This is a "move" handle. If you grab it with a left click of your mouse, you can drag it anywhere you want. Clicking it will select your entire table so you can format it. Try moving your table with the "move" handle. Go ahead! Try it!

TIP: Before you insert a graphic or table, hit the "Enter" key a few times to pad space. MS Office Programs tend to respond better when you have space "padded out" inside your document.

Table Tools Tab

Clicking inside a table will cause the Table Tools Tabs appear at the far right of your ribbon. Table Tools include the Design and Layout Tabs.

Design Tab   Layout Tab

Fig 12 – Table Tools Tabs

The table tools tab appears when you select a table. The Design tab is for Color and Appearance while the Layout Tab is for layout, merging or splitting cells and other layout options.

The Design Tab

The design tab allows the selection of colors, insertion or deletion of columns or rows and inclusion or exclusion of table options.

Table Style Options Group

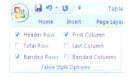 Table style options are used in connection with the table style group in the Design Tab.

Fig 13 – Design Tab – Table Style Options

Table style options are used when you are trying to eliminate specific table styles.   Unchecking each box will remove those options from your selection list.

Table Styles Group

Fig 14 Table Styles Group Allows you to choose a variety of colors, lines and other design options.

The *"Table styles"* group allows you to choose colors, bands, lines and other options for your new table.   **Style** and **Design** are used interchangeably in a lot of text books.

Draw Borders Group

The "Draw Borders" group on the "Design" Tab allows you to choose border styles. They can be solid, really thin, thick, dashed, dotted and the colors can be changed.

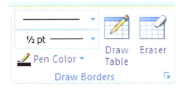

Draw Borders allows the selection of pen color, drawing tables, pen colors, etc

Fig 15 – Draw Borders Group in Design Tab

The Layout Tab

Select your table and you will see the design and layout tabs to the right.   Select the Layout Tab.

Fig 16 – Ribbon with the Layout Tab

Table Group

The first group on the left is the "*Table*" group.   This allows you to view and select various cells on the table and display table gridlines.

Fig 17 – The Table group at the far left of the ribbon

Rows & Columns Group

Second from the left is the Rows and Columns tab. You can add rows, columns or delete rows and columns.

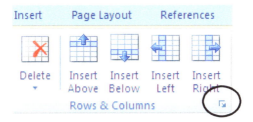

Fig 18 - Rows & Columns Group on the Layout Tab

The tiny button on the lower right is the Table Insert Cells menu. It has the same options as the Rows and Columns group.

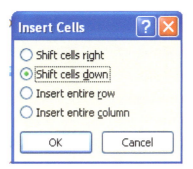

Fig 19: Table Insert Cells Menu

The Merge Group

The next group is the "*Merge*" group. This allows you to either merge or split cells and tables. It is useful if you want to display information like tables and figures in a book, paper or publication.

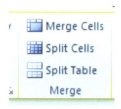

Fig 20: The Merge Group

The Cell Size Group

You can resize row height, column width, or automatically fit your cell size to the text that you type in it. Selecting Distribute Rows or Distribute Columns causes MS Word to evenly space your rows or columns across or up and down your page.

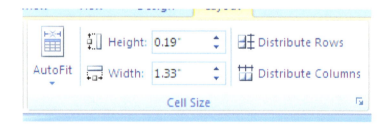

Fig 21 – Cell Size Group

Alignment Group

The alignment group allows you to change text direction, cell alignment and cell margins. You can adjust how your text or graphics will align with the alignment buttons.   This is useful when you create reports that need information placed precisely.

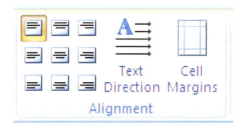

Fig 22: Alignment Group allows specific alignment of single cells or groups of cells.

Data Group

The data group allows you to sort contents of a table, convert the contents of a table to text and allows you do perform simple math and logic tasks.

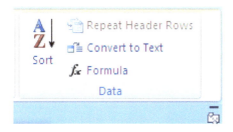

Fig 23: Data group allows sorting, conversion and formulas

Removing Border Lines

This is a caution symbol with an earth graphic in the center.

Fig 24 – A Table

Figure 24 is exactly the same as **Figure 4**.   What is missing? **The lines**!   You do not need border lines on a table.   As you can see from figure 4, it looks much cleaner than the one with the lines.

At the Home Tab of either 2007 or 2010, in the Paragraph group, you should be able to find the Borders and shading button.

Step 1, Select the entire table by selecting the "move handle" (Figure 9). The borders and shading button is in the Paragraph group. There should be an arrow just to the right of that button.   Click the arrow.

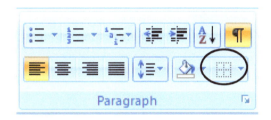

The paragraph Group –Borders and Shading.

Step 2, you should see a menu. Notice that a lot of the selections are highlighted.   Select the "No Border" option. If you still have a border, try again.

Borders and Shading Menu. To remove all the borders, select **"No Border"**

Clarifying Exercises

Exercise 1 – A Contribution Statement

You work for an agency that needs to send a report about contributors. Below is a contribution statement. The company name is "**For the Children**".

Contribution Statement

Contributor A	$5,000.00	1/2/2011
Contributor B	$7,500.00	2/2/2011
Contributor C	$9,000.00	2/2/2011
Contributor D	$4,500.00	2/3/2011

Insert the Table

Step 1 – Insert your table. There are five rows you need to insert and three columns – one column for each item of information. Insert a 3 x 5 table.

Step 2 – Type your information into the table

Contribution statement		
Contributor A	$5,000.00	1/2/2011
Contributor B	$7,500.00	2/2/2011
Contributor C	$9,000.00	2/2/2011
Contributor D	$4,500.00	2/3/2011

Your boss wants the words "Contribution Statement" centered over the entire table and each column needs a heading.

Insert Rows Below

Step 3 – Select the top Row, right click the top row and select Insert.

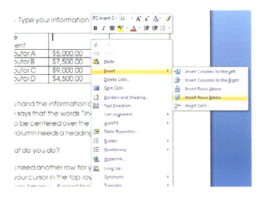

Step 4: Select Insert Rows Below.   This will add a row directly below the "Contribution Statement" part of your table.

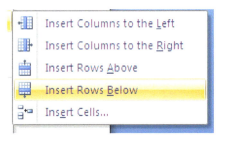

Contribution statement		
Contributor A	$5,000.00	1/2/2011
Contributor B	$7,500.00	2/2/2011
Contributor C	$9,000.00	2/2/2011
Contributor D	$4,500.00	2/3/2011

Step 5: Type in your column headings – then bold them.

Contribution statement		
Name	**Amount**	**Date**
Contributor A	$5,000.00	1/2/2011
Contributor B	$7,500.00	2/2/2011
Contributor C	$9,000.00	2/2/2011
Contributor D	$4,500.00	2/3/2011

Merge a Row

Step 6: Select / Highlight the entire First Row

Contribution statement¤	¤	¤
Name¤	Amount¤	Date¤

Step 7: With the first row selected, click the Layout Tab.

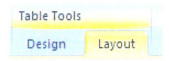

Step 8: Find the "Merge" group and select "Merge Cells".

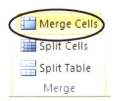

Contribution statement		
Name	**Amount**	**Date**
Contributor A	$5,000.00	1/2/2011
Contributor B	$7,500.00	2/2/2011
Contributor C	$9,000.00	2/2/2011
Contributor D	$4,500.00	2/3/2011

Center the Contents of Your Merged Row

With your cursor still inside the top row, find the "Alignment Group and select the "center" button.   This will vertically and horizontally align your information.

The Alignment Group in the Layout Tab

Contribution statement		
Name	Amount	Date
Contributor A	$5,000.00	1/2/2011
Contributor B	$7,500.00	2/2/2011
Contributor C	$9,000.00	2/2/2011
Contributor D	$4,500.00	2/3/2011

Insert a Column and Merge Cells

Your boss likes your design.   She would *really* like to see the company logo in a column on the left and the text direction to be vertical.

Step 1: Insert a column to the left of the first column. To do this, you need to select the first column on the left.

Contribution·statement¤		
Name¤	**Amount¤**	**Date¤**
Contributor·A¤	$5,000.00¤	1/2/2011¤
Contributor·B¤	$7,500.00¤	2/2/2011¤
Contributor·C¤	$9,000.00¤	2/2/2011¤
Contributor·D¤	$4,500.00¤	2/3/2011¤

Step 2: Select the Layout Tab and go to the Rows & Columns Group.   Select the "Insert Left" button.

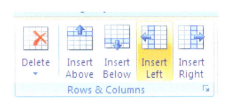

Contribution statement		
Name	Amount	Date
Contributor A	$5,000.00	1/2/2011
Contributor B	$7,500.00	2/2/2011
Contributor C	$9,000.00	2/2/2011
Contributor D	$4,500.00	2/3/2011

Step 3: Select the entire first column, but **NOT** the top row.

Contribution statement		
Name	Amount	Date
Contributor A	$5,000.00	1/2/2011
Contributor B	$7,500.00	2/2/2011
Contributor C	$9,000.00	2/2/2011
Contributor D	$4,500.00	2/3/2011

Step 4: Select "Merge Cells" From the Merge Group.

	Contribution statement		
	Name	Amount	Date
	Contributor A	$5,000.00	1/2/2011
	Contributor B	$7,500.00	2/2/2011
	Contributor C	$9,000.00	2/2/2011
	Contributor D	$4,500.00	2/3/2011

Step 5: Select the top Row.

¤	Contribution·statement¤		
¤	Name¤	Amount¤	Date¤
	Contributor	$5,000.00~	1/2/2011~

Step 6: Select "*Merge Cells*" in the *Merge* Group.

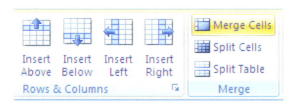

Contribution statement			
	Name	Amount	Date
	Contributor A	$5,000.00	1/2/2011
	Contributor B	$7,500.00	2/2/2011
	Contributor C	$9,000.00	2/2/2011
	Contributor D	$4,500.00	2/3/2011

Enter text and change text direction

Your boss wants the name of the company "For the Children" to be in *Lucida Calligraphy*.

Step 1: Type the full text of the company name in the newly merged cell in column 1.

Contribution statement			
For The Children	Name	Amount	Date
	Contributor A	$5,000.00	1/2/2011
	Contributor B	$7,500.00	2/2/2011
	Contributor C	$9,000.00	2/2/2011
	Contributor D	$4,500.00	2/3/2011

Step 2: Select/Highlight the text you just typed.

Contribution statement¤			
For·The·Children¤	Name¤	Amount¤	Date¤
	Contributor A	$5,000.00¤	1/2/2011¤

Step 3: Select the Alignment group under the Layout Tab. Select "**Text Direction**"

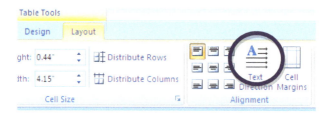

Step 4: Click the Text Direction button until you get the desired direction. Then change the font to Lucida Calligraphy

Be sure to experiment with text direction so you can get an idea of how it works.

Contribution statement			
For The Children	Name	Amount	Date
	Contributor A	$5,000.00	1/2/2011
	Contributor B	$7,500.00	2/2/2011
	Contributor C	$9,000.00	2/2/2011
	Contributor D	$4,500.00	2/3/2011

Graphics

Graphic Types

Graphics are useful for delivering ideas quickly. Some of the more common graphic formats are listed below[2].

Graphic Type	Description	Pros & Cons
Bitmaps	A format used in storing images. Each bit of the picture is mapped into pixels.	Has greater visual accuracy but tends to be very large
GIF	A compressed format for storing images. Similar to JPEGs.	A good in-between format from bitmap to vector. Very common format.
JPEG	Graphic formats for storing compressed images.	Smaller image size but gets fuzzy when sized to large.
PNG	(portable network graphic)A format for encoding a picture pixel by pixel and sending it over the web	Does not take up too much room and delivers good quality.
SVG	(Scalable Vector Graphic) - XML-language for describing 2D-graphics	Used in a web based language (XML)
Vectors	A vector graphic uses a linear calculation (vector) to define the appearance of an image.	Smaller than Bitmaps, but good for scalable images
WMF	Windows Metafile – For use between Windows Programs	For exchange between Windows Programs.

What is clipart?

The term clipart hearkens back to pre-digital copy art. The copy artists would literally clip art out of a printed page and paste the art where they wanted it to appear. The artwork was pasted in the desired location using wax. This allowed for operator error. Digital clipart is similar, but without the scissors or the wax.

Clipart used to be in pages that were clipped out with scissors or a razor blade.

Inserting Graphics

In 2007 as well as 2010, graphics are placed with the "insert" tab.

Pictures, clipart, shapes, smart art, charts or screenshots may be placed in most Microsoft documents

The really cool thing about 2010 is the screenshot option where you can insert a graphic of any open window of your computer. This is great if you need to document a process or event.

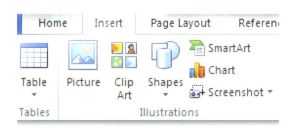

Inserting Clipart

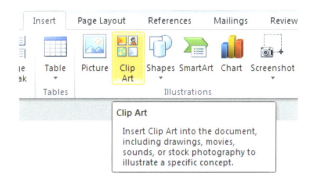

Step 1: Select the Insert tab in MS Word. Look to the Illustrations group. Press the Clip Art Button. A Clip Art Menu should appear at the far right.

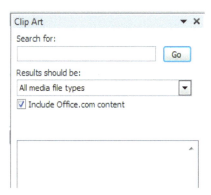

Step 2: In the Search For: box, type the word "computer" and select the "GO" button. You should get results similar to what is pictured below. If you are asked to search the web, select the "Yes" button. This will expand your search.

Select the "Yes" button to search the web.

Screen tip with indexing

Hovering over individual clipart will reveal a screen tip. You should also see a drop down arrow. When you click the drop down arrow, you will see a menu similar to the one below. Select "insert".

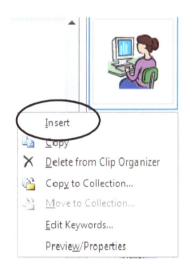

Resize and Rotate Graphics/Clipart

When you insert the image, you should see circles on each corner and in the middle of each side of the graphic. Each circle is a handle.

The handles allow you to grab your clipart using your left mouse button. Selecting the corner handle and moving it up or down allows you to resize your graphic while keeping the aspect.

Aspect is what makes pictures look normal. If you grab a handle that is on either vertical side, you will change the picture's horizontal aspect. The picture will stretch out and become elongated.

Graphic Handles

Graphic stretched horizontally

If you grab a handle on one of the horizontal sides and pull upward, your picture stretches vertically.

Graphic stretched vertically

The rotate handle

By grabbing the green handle, you can rotate any image you insert into MS Office 360 degrees. You may also use the "Rotate" button in the Picture > Format Tab.

Partially rotated image

Graphic Behavior

Graphics, whatever they may be, have specific behaviors. Some types of graphics, such as Windows Meta Files allow quite a bit of flexibility within the MS Office Document.

It is important to understand graphic behavior so that appropriate placement can be done for each graphic.

When you have selected a graphic, you will see a "Picture Tools" tab appear on the MS Ribbon. This gives you a variety of options on how to handle your newly inserted graphic.

Since we have inserted a Windows Metafile (*.wmf), we will explore the options available.

Picture Tools Tab

In the Arrange Group. Click the "Wrap Text" button.

The Arrange Group

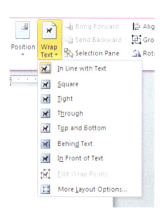

Notice the options that control its behavior. The different graphics you insert into your document will determine what graphic format options will appear.

Graphic Behavior Options

Here are illustrations of the different behavior options.

In Line With Text	You can easily change the formatting of selected text from the Quick Styles gallery on the... ther controls o... n the Home... urrent theme or using a format that you spe...	**Top and Bottom**	u can easily change the formatting of s... ed text from the Quick Styles gallery or... r controls on the Home tab. Most cont... sing a format that you specify directly.
Square	an easily change the formatting of s... text from the Quick Styles gallery or controls from the curr overall look of b. To change ent Quick St lery provide reset commands so that	**Behind Text**	l text from the Quick Styles gallery on... controls on... Most contr... ng a format that you sp... fy directly. T ments of the Page Layout tab. To cha Current Q... ommand. Bo ommands so that... always restc our current template. ¶
Tight	easily change the formatting of t from the Quick Styles gallery trols on the theme of your do ge the loo Set comma ommands so that you can alwa	**In Front of Text**	xt from the Quick Styles gallery on ntrols on Most contr a forma fy directly. T ents or ttab. To cha urrent C ommand. Bc mands so always rest ar current template. ¶
Through	an easily change the formatting o text from the Quick Styles gallery ontrols on the nt theme ok of your do ange the loo yle Set comma t commands so that you can alwa		

Behaviors may look very similar, but remember that they are useful for specific layouts.

You can change the behavior of your graphics with the position button. The Position button is right next to the Wrap Text button

The position menu

Tables, Merging and Graphics

Exercise 2 – Totaling Numbers (adding)

You work for **Komaru Enterprises**. Komaru Enterprises produces a report that has the following numbers.
To begin, create a table similar to the one below. If it isn't exactly the same, that's great because creativity helps learning.

Make sure the numbers agree so you can check your answers.

Komaru Enterprises Report		
Region	**Expenses**	**Sales**
Central	125,000.00	246,021.00
Western	100,000.00	160,000.00
Eastern	56,500.00	120,000.00
Totals		

What we will be doing with this table.

- Total the columns under Expenses and Sales

Creating Totals

Place your cursor in the blank cell below the expenses in the totals row.

Step 1: Select the Formula Button on the table Layout Tab

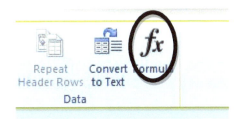

Step 2: You should see a menu similar to the one below

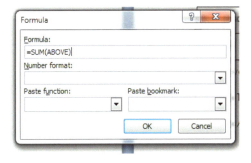

What Microsoft has done is guess what you want to do. It thinks you want to sum the column above your cell. *Good Guess Microsoft!*

Step 3: Select the number format from the drop down and press "OK".

The total should appear at the bottom of that column

Totals¤	281500.00¤	¤

Try the same process for the next column.

Totals¤	281500.00¤	526021.00¤

Exercise3 – Inserting Screen Print into a table

For this exercise, you need to find the "Print screen" button or buttons.   On a laptop, you may have to press a "Fn" key and a PRTSC key.   Check your computer's instruction manual on how to do this.

Step 1: Insert a table.   Usually, I insert a single column with two rows.   This gives me the option of deleting the second row and conserving space when I have to.

Step 2: Take a screen shot of your computer.   I would suggest you start with a print screen of your desktop.

Step 3: Open up Microsoft Paint. We are just going to clip a piece of the screen.
 Start >All Programs> Accessories > Paint

Step 4: With MS Paint open, select Paste or Press **CTRL + V**

You should see your desktop inside MS Paint.

As you hover over the picture inside MS Paint, you should see a cursor that points in four different directions.

Step 5: Left click and move the picture around until you see the white background in MS Paint.

Step 6: Click in the white space and then draw a square around a portion of your computer screen graphic in MS Paint. Use the precision select pointer.

Step 7: Right Click and then select "**COPY**".

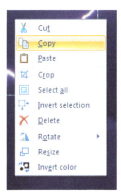

Step 8a: Select the top row of your table.

Step 8b: Select "PASTE".

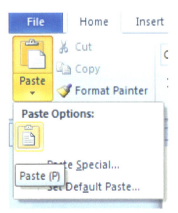

Your partial screen shot should appear in the table. If you want to be a great picture placement specialist, you should pay close attention to detail.   For example, did you notice how it aligned to the left inside the table cell?   This is the default option that MS Word gives the graphic object. If you click inside the table and select your "Layout" options, you can align this graphic using the alignment group.

Align Your Screen Shot

Your screen shot is aligned left.   In order to center it within the table, you would select your table and then the "Layout" tab of the Table Tools Tab.

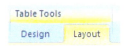

Table Tools >
Layout Tab

Refer to **page 24** for alignment options. Then, align your screen shot to center. Select the cell you want to align, select table tools > Layout and then select the center button.

Fit Your Image to the Table

Table functions in MS Word allow you to resize your table to fit your inserted object.

Step 1: click inside the table and select the Table Layout Tab.

Step 2: Select the "Autofit" button in the "Merge" group.

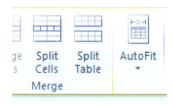

Step 3: Select AutoFit Contents.

Your table should now be tightly around your graphic. Please note that your table will shift over to the left. If you want it centered, go to the Home Tab and select the Align Center button and your table should be centered.

The advantage to this is that you can do a lot of editing to your graphic and you will still have picture perfect placement because it is now in a table.

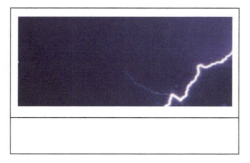

Refer to Page 24 if you wish to see the alignment function. Refer to page 26 if you wish to remove the borders from the table, or make some slick designs of your own.

Exercise 4 - Create a Monthly Report

For this exercise, you need to understand how Mail Merge works. If you do not understand this process, you might want to go to the Internet and search for Mail Merge, or you could buy my book "Mail Merge Explained: All About Lists" at http://www.amazon.com/

Your boss has a letter with a table that he wants to use for a monthly income report. The format needs to stay the same, but the numbers change.

The letter is appropriately formatted. For this exercise, we will focus on how to insert merge fields into the table.

Sales By Division and Department			
Division	Dept A	Dept B	Dept C
Div A			
Div B			
Totals			

You have created a database with the following information. Edit your entries as needed.

You need the department totals for Depts. A B and C.

You have started mail merge and you will be inserting the division Totals for each department. This is for reference purposes and clarity. Your department names will vary.

Sales By Division and Department			
Division	Dept A	Dept B	Dept C
Div A	«DIV_A_DEPT_A»	«DIV_A_DEPT_B»	«DIV_A_DEPT_C»
Div B	«DIV_B_DEPT_A»	«DIV_B_DEPT_B»	«DIV_B_DEPT_C»
Totals	0.00	0.00	$ 0.00

After this, you will insert totals into the tables. Select the Department "A" column and then select the **Table Tools > Layout Tab.**

In the data group, insert =Sum(ABOVE) and this will total all the numbers above that cell.

If you show your unprintable characters and toggle your field codes, your table should look like this.

Sales By Division and Department ¤			
Division ¤	Dept ·A¤	Dept ·B¤	Dept ·C¤
Div ·A¤	«DIV_A_DEPT_A»¤	«DIV_A_DEPT_B»¤	«DIV_A_DEPT_C»¤
Div ·B¤	«DIV_B_DEPT_A»¤	«DIV_B_DEPT_B»¤	«DIV_B_DEPT_C»¤
Totals¤	{=SUM(ABOVE) · \# ·"#,##0.00"·}¤	{=SUM(ABOVE) · \# ·"#,##0.00"·}¤	{=SUM(ABOVE) · \# · "$#,##0.00;($#, ##0.00)"·}¤

Right click each total field and select "Update Record". Your table should now look like the picture below when you select "Preview Results" in your Mail Merge group.

Sales By Division and Department ¤			
Division ·¤	Dept ·A¤	Dept ·B¤	Dept ·C¤
Div ·A¤	213000¤	213000¤	120000¤
Div ·B¤	123000¤	234000¤	123000¤
Totals¤	336,000.00¤	447,000.00¤	$243,000.00¤

All you have to do is change the numbers and the dates, and you look like a champ in the office.

Reference and Citations

No one creates an intellectual work alone.   There are many contributors, but one writer.   Thanks to all those who had information that was useful in producing this work.

Citation List

1. http://www.shaunakelly.com/word/concepts/tables.html
2. http://www.w3schools.com/w3c/w3c_other.asp